# DEAR DARLING

# DEAR DARLING

## THE GOLDEN EDITION

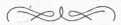

A COLLECTION OF
POETRY & PROSE

+

BY

### FREYDIS LOVA

FREYDIS LOVA POETRY

2022

# TABLE OF CONTENTS

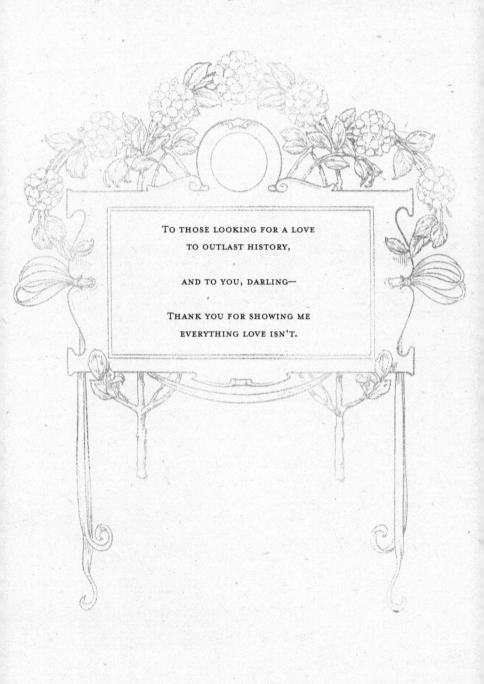

TO THOSE LOOKING FOR A LOVE
TO OUTLAST HISTORY,

AND TO YOU, DARLING—

THANK YOU FOR SHOWING ME
EVERYTHING LOVE ISN'T.

I've often found that when poets write about love—
especially a lost or failed love— they compare
themselves to birds who have had their wings clipped.
Poor souls who have been thrown into a cage and live
with the devil they know because they're familiar. As
much as this image is used, I still find it to be one of
the most beautiful visuals to exist. You see, every cage
is different. Some are ornate and lavish, while others
are small and rusting away.

Mine was a mad combination of the two. I was not
a songbird with a tied beak, nor was I a pretty little
thing with clipped wings. I was a canary in a coal
mine— unaware of what was happening until it was
almost too late. He let me sing freely, but over time, I
lost my lyrics and chirped out his tunes, helping him
in his selfish quest with no regard for myself. I could
fly as I pleased, sweeping up and down the shafts in
darkness, adapting to the danger as it came, but he
would become mad if I flew too far up on my own.
And when I fell, I fell into a false love, until one day, I
looked around and saw that the glimmering lie he had
so graciously gifted me was nothing but fool's gold—
tarnished to soot and dust.

The words that fill the following pages began as
silent conversations between myself and an empty
apartment. Although, if I'm being completely honest,
there was another in the apartment with me. He
was there physically, but his mind and body were
with others. He was there emotionally, sometimes,
although I quickly found anger instead of love. He
was there for everyone except for me— until I tried
to leave. I found my peace on the frequent occasions
when he was gone, making friends with the ghosts of
what we once were in hopes that they would come back
to life.

Eventually, I realized that I was casting my dreams
into a hollow night sky. The sparrows had swept away

the stardust, and the ravens had no more room to carry wishes on their wings. As time crept on, they carried my voice away with them, as I was too tired to continue to have the same pleading conversation time after time again with a boy pretending to listen, pretending to change, pretending to be a man, failing to be a partner.

It was then that I began to write. Everything I wanted to say, everything that I was too scared to say, found a home on scraps of paper, corners of notebooks, and Polaroid pictures that no longer held any meaning to me. When I left, I took these words with me— the sole souvenir from years of being lost and silenced. Now, I share these words with you.

*Freydis*

Acer saccharum

Falling

There was something romantic about the day—
how the sun was high in the sky,
a cornflower blue after the storm
that shook the Spanish roof tiles
to the rhythm of the thunder from the night before.

The air was heavy in a way that I welcomed.
Perhaps the struggle to breathe was only nerves.
But the sun beat down on fallen palm leaves,
and soft jazz billowed from my car windows
out into the parking lot, expanding the
small refuge of shade and comfort in front of
an unfamiliar door. This was what the
Hollywood films prepared me for.

I had spent so long dreaming, so long hoping,
and then, suddenly, I was in a place where
magic poured from every dilapidated apartment,
and every cliché stood in line to kiss the willing
without embarrassment or regret.

We were a generation of believers,
ready to be hurt and stand tall in the rubble,
because every photograph snapped with
our blinking eyes under starlit street signs
would be one step closer to reaching the sun—

that sun. Pounding down on freckled shoulders.
There was something romantic about the day.

And then I saw you.

You walked past my apartment,
shirt tucked in and hair slicked back.
One of my roommates did a double take
and asked the rest of us if we had seen you.

I looked past her shoulder and said,
*Oh. That's just* ~~████████~~

Maybe that was my first mistake—
saying your name.
It rolled off my tongue kind of effortlessly.

And I liked the sound of it.

That's how it started:
with your name.
It was like you had heard it
through the sliding glass door.

Like it was pounding to get out,
banging until the barrier between us
slid open and you could hear me.

One name. An impartial passing comment.
I only knew you from social media.
We had talked maybe two or three times,
but our conversations were never long.

I never expected to meet you in person—
you seemed too preoccupied.
But there you were, reaching for your phone,
standing in front of my car before unlocking yours,
right next to it, then getting in and driving off.

My screen lit up as my phone pinged.

Five girls squealed with excitement.

They convinced me to respond immediately.

You liked the way I dressed.
Petticoats and A-line dresses
hugging my figure above my waist,
cinching it in with a belt in the middle.
*Soft bombshell curves*, is what you called them.

You liked how I wore my hair
in Hollywood waves, or tucked back
in a chignon, or low back roll with a scarf.
*Timeless beauty*, is what you called it.

You liked how I did my makeup—
eyeliner, thin and black— a small cat eye in the corner.
Red lips, smudge-proof and glossy.
I always filled in the mole on my cheek
after covering it with foundation,
but I kept my freckles hidden away.
*Perfect*, is what you called me.

You never said anything about my personality.

Even still, you somehow managed to carry
the dreaming of the first day over
into every day that followed. With you,
I romanticized the mundane things.

Waking up before the sun to a blaring alarm.
Getting dressed in the walk-in closet as to not
wake my roommate. Putting my face on as quietly
as I possibly could to hide the bags beneath my eyes.

I did my hair in the car after parking.
Rollers found a new home in a bag on my
passenger's seat while I danced through my shifts.
You thought it was cute. I thought it was too much effort.

But I never stopped, because it was fitting for me
to walk around a boulevard set in the 1940s,
twirling at random times and singing along
with the area loop. Forty-five minutes of harmonizing.

Then another forty-five.

And then another.

*It's the vintage style*, you said.

Another forty-five minutes.

I never expected you to join me.

You were only a dancer when everyone was watching.
You did it for the attention, whereas I danced
because I loved the music. I would choreograph
foxtrots and waltzes in my mind, picturing old film stars
making their way down the street and through empty shops
in one of those dream sequences where everyone fades out,
only to have the male lead snap back into reality and realize
he's been standing there, in the middle of a crowd,
getting honked at by a car horn because he needs to finish
crossing the street. Sometimes I would imagine myself
doing these dances, but who my partner was, I couldn't say.

I never saw their face. Only a silhouette that you didn't fit.

If Ginger Rogers could dance
backwards in heels, so can I.

But I refuse to let myself be lead
back in time. I want to dance through life.

It was a purple sundress kind of day.
You know the one—
where the humidity is high
but you're going out with friends
so you feel the pressure to look
cute, but not too dressed up,
while also being practical.

There was nothing practical about us,
our little group of misfits.
None of us seemed to fit anywhere,
so we decided to fit together.

*And for a moment, it was wonderful.*

Someone pause the movie.
I want to remember
how everyone is
in this exact moment,
before the screen statics out
and the reel is ruined.

It's Valentine's Day,
and while everyone is hoping
to be struck with Cupid's arrow,
I'm off shooting archery
and bouncing around with bears.

I wouldn't have it any other way.

I clock out and see
a slew of messages from you.
All I want after today
is a moment of peace.

I join you and our friends
for a horror movie marathon.

You had never had *Whoppers* before.
You loved to drink malts, but you
never had them in candy form.
So I shared my box with you during the movie,
and everyone laughed lovingly as you gasped,
acting as though you had just discovered
the most amazing thing in the world,
right before it would disappeared forever.

*Let's go someplace,*
you said. And I agreed
because the night was young
and so was I,
and I thought that was how life was.

Our little chosen family
piled up on each other—
a mess of arms wrapping
around someone else,
trying to sneak in between
other bodies. We had a love
for each other that was starved—

and I was nothing but bone.

Parisian music played softly
around the pillars in the courtyard.
The stars were twinkling, and the
strangers who moved around us
were polite, acting like they didn't see us.
You stayed behind a bit,
waiting for them. And I looked back,
eager to know who they were.

You hugged them tightly,
arms lingering around one of them,
and I smiled, because that was the happiest
I had seen you since we had met.

She called you, sobbing, as we were leaving.
Not the one we knew you were crushing on,
but someone else. Another soul who trusted you.

I sat in the car with a friend of yours
and listened as he went off,
telling me that I didn't have a chance
with you. How you had too many other girls
you flirted with, and how even though
you were playful, you had your sights set
on the one you refused to introduce us to.

I raised a brow and chuckled,
which I think confused him.

*Is this your reputation?*
I thought.

*I'm not interested in him like that.*
I answered, somewhat to your friend's relief.
*Not romantically. But thanks for the warning.*

How I wish those words stayed true.

It was about a week
before I saw you again.
Work became crazy,
as it often does
after settling into
a comfortable routine.

You looked for me—
or at least that's what you told me—
when you knew I was around
and you were on shift.

So why did you rush away
and hide in the back room
when you saw me with him?

He liked that I drank beer,
and I liked that he had a sense of humor.

He liked how my hand felt in his,
and I liked how he kissed me during the fireworks.

He liked how smart I was,
and I liked how he wanted to keep learning.

You liked how we never tried
to say *hi* to you again
after you ran off that first time.

Midnight drives under hurricane skies,
grey clouds composed symphonies, warming up
for their next show. Conducted by wind,
rain ruined sheet music. Ink ran
with bare feet to shelter, blue and black
smudges smeared staves and the corners of
eyes, crinkled with laughter. The parking lot
was a world wide, the light from
the still-standing street lamps, golden.
We waited out the storm together,
front row seats to a simple spring shower.
Puddle-drenched shoes were tossed carelessly into the
back seat as we wrung out our shirts,
sticking to skin that had yet to be sun-kissed.

And then the morning came.

And you saw me come home,
walking down the little path
with my sandals hanging by my side
and a smile on my lips before
the first sign of dawn touched the ends
of the sky. Wild curls and running makeup—
I was a disaster, and yet, I had never felt
more beautiful and at peace.

I waved to you as you drove to work.
Your eyes met mine, but you ignored me.
I left the twinge of pain I felt on the
other side of the door as I crept
off to bed, exhausted from the storm.

You were nervous around me after that—
wringing your hands or keeping them in your pockets.
You looked down at your boots, and if you weren't
so invested in your appearance, I bet you would have
scuffed them against the pavement to distract yourself
from everything that wasn't going in your favor.

I didn't come around
with him anymore.
You came to see me at my job
a few times, but didn't stay
when you found out he was on shift.

If you had—
if you had even talked to me—
you would've given me the chance
to tell you that it didn't work out.
That we were just friends.

Instead, you chose to live in a fantasy
where I could only ever be yours
when we were away from everyone else.

Funny— I don't remember agreeing to be a part of that.

Tell me, Darling,

how many sunrises
did you watch on Sunset
and see me, displaced
from that half-formed memory
and onto your soundstage,
where I was coming home to you?

I remember when you told me
you had decided to start going
with her. How excited you were
for your first date, and how
I smiled and told you
how happy I was for you. And I
was, truly, happy for you.
You were my friend, and she
was gorgeous, and kind, and
had a soul that shone so brightly,
it illuminated everything good hidden by
your tarnished light that blinded
everyone around you. Maybe
that's why it stopped working so quickly —
you knew that she was too good for you.

And Darling, she still is.

Everything went back to the way it was after that.
I would plan your dates for you,
slipping you ideas and eagerly waiting to be caught up
on what had happened the night before.
To find out which song you sang to her.
If you danced on the beach after the fireworks ended
and everyone cleared out, not knowing they piped in
old Elvis songs through hidden speakers.

I think that part of you knew that these were dates
I would have loved to take someone on.
But if I wasn't going to have the chance to use them,
someone else should— and I knew she would appreciate them.

We held parties in laundry rooms
at three in the morning. Our
small group would gather, baskets
on hips and bags slung over shoulders.
Candy wrappers littered benches
between sunburnt thighs as we passed
half-empty bottles of wine and tequila
around, the dull hum of worn-down
machines serving as background music.

Propose with a ring pop. Exchange
chocolate bars for a dowery.
I'll officiate the ceremony happening,
not out of love, but as a treaty
between the one who was always prepared
and the one who needed to borrow someone's
fabric softener. Not out of love, we laughed,
slipping on wet floors and fighting washers for
our quarters back. Not out of love.

*Not out of love.*

Maybe not the romantic kind, at least,
but there was love there, once.
In those moments, under harsh lights
and surrounded by damp smells
and missing socks, eaten by machines—
whose funerals were always so lovely—
there was a family. There was love.

And more often than not,
I wish it had stayed that way.

We shared dirty jokes
and secrets, plans for the future,
our deepest desires.

*I want french fries.*
*And a milkshake.*

You laughed— something
you had been doing less of lately—
and said that sounded good.

But I didn't want to be alone with you
and a heavy silence, so six of us
piled into a booth at the closest
pancake house, and ordered breakfast
at one-thirty in the morning
along with a side of fries and milkshakes.

It almost felt normal.

You watched as I dipped a fry into my milkshake,
coating the greasy wedge with melting chocolate.

*Have you never dipped a fry in a milkshake before?*

It was an innocent enough question,
but you looked like I had insulted everyone you loved.

I pushed my basket of fries toward you.
You took one and dipped it into your malt,
popping it into your mouth and pausing.

*There* was that genuine, blissful smile we all missed.

A scalloped collar that hung
off my shoulders. A cinched waist
and an A-line skirt that fluttered
around my knees when I walked,
or danced down the sidewalk,
or swayed when I stood in place,
waiting for someone to follow.
Black and white heels brought me
from tile to tile, skipping cracks
in the concrete. A simple watch
on my wrist, and no one on my arm.

Just because my lips were red
didn't mean I was looking
for someone to kiss.

Every little girl wants a princess moment.
I had mine when we were on the ferry.
I peered out over the banister
and looked up to the sky,
in awe of the stars
and how visible they were that night.
My hair was a mess of curls,
and the light was just right.

I saw you looking at me,
and that's when I realized
that I wasn't a little girl,
and I didn't want a to be a princess.

Late night conversations
in parking lots with friends,
stealing glances across empty
spaces, or over dashboards, or through
rolled-down windows. You said,
*Let's go for a drive. Just us.*
and I said, *No.* I was happy
enough under a few stars and a
vast sky, sharing silent stories
with two other souls as we
waited for the sun to rise.

But then you pushed,
and I became uncomfortable.
Our friends were more vocal
about how you had feelings for me.
About how they weren't feelings of friendship.
I tried to ignore them. I tried to distance
myself
from
you.
But you kept coming back,
and I knew I had no choice
but to build a barrier
between our apartment doors.

*Why are you doing this?*

You froze. When I asked if we could talk,
I think you were expecting some
undying love confession from me.

Not this.

*Why are you treating her like this?*

You refused to look at me.
Even still, your body language said it all.

*You don't do this to someone you love.*
*It isn't fair to her. Isn't fair to anyone.*

You let it all spill out then,
and I wish, still to this day,
that you had choked on the vile
you spewed up instead.

I left you there,
the first time,
standing alone
under the street light
that guided the park's pathway
between our front doors.
I told you I wouldn't wait
for you to fall out of love
with her. You told me
you never were in love with her,
and somehow, that was worse
than being asked to stand in line.

*Stay golden.*

Two little words, so silly,
looking back on them now.

**Stay**
/stā/

*Verb*

*Remain in the same place; Remain in a specific state or position.*

**Golden**
/ˈgōldən/

*Adjective*

*Colored or shining like gold; Made or consisting of gold.*

When I think back on that night,
which isn't often at all,
everything is blurred.
Your face and the sadness I thought
I once saw fill your eyes
when I told you I wasn't playing
your selfish, childish games.
I don't remember what time it was—
only that it was dark.
I don't remember what we were wearing—
but I do remember donating the outfit
after I couldn't wash the pain I felt
for myself out of the seams
the next day. And now, I can't even
remember your voice, or what you said.
There's a part of me that thinks
you didn't say anything at all.
That you knew I had you figured out,
and that you couldn't say anything
because you knew you couldn't lie to me
any more than you already had.

I do remember one part of that night, though.
I told you to *stay golden,*
as though my words would somehow
take the rusting facade you so proudly wore,
and turn it into something honorable.

You stood there, drowning
in your thoughts as I walked away.
I wondered if you would come after me.
I didn't want you to chase me.
I didn't want to be your second choice,
brought forth by regret, by the thought of loss.
I refused to be trapped in your suffocating light.

I am a wildflower who thrives
beneath silver strands sent from the moon.
Maybe that's why I did it at night.
Maybe I needed her strength to help me.
Or maybe I wanted to make it poetic,
so that when you woke up the next morning,
it would feel as though it— as though I—
was nothing but a dream.

We stopped talking then—
for a few days, anyway.
Our friends reached out to me,
wanting to know why
you were suddenly singing
such sad songs.
I was foolish enough to listen,
to take in each melancholy note
as though it were the sweetest
chocolate, your whines, the
smoothest Pinot Noir.
You helped me get drunk
on your disasters, and when
you had me there, comforting you
like the beautiful fool I was—
although, at the time,
you only called me beautiful—
I sang along. And you were happy.

If you ever truly loved me,
you would have let me live
in sinlence.

The laundry room parties stopped then.
I still did my wash on Wednesdays, though,
when the facility was empty and the night was high.
You walked in as I was piling my clothes
into the dryer, and stood behind me without a word.

I asked you how you were doing.
You never did laundry on Wednesdays anymore.
You said you were healing.

I miss the naive girl who thought that
our slates had been washed clean
along with dirty uniforms and favorite shirts.

*Let's go for a drive.*

*Just the two of us.*

Stupidly, I said, Yes.

You cried that night.

We pulled into the parking lot at work—
the only safe space you could think of.
A few cars staggered here and there
from the night shift.
Statues stuck in a paved-over garden,
ready to be removed before dawn.

Nothing flourishes in concrete cracks here.
Not even weeds.

Another silence came
when you told me you had ended things with her.
I pretended I didn't know.
I pretended I wasn't talking to my best friend
in the apartment complex parking lot
when we saw you, and how you stood there
after she drove away. I pretended
that I wasn't encouraged to comfort you.
To talk to you about it. But every time
we had a serious talk, it ended with me
leaving you alone under a solitary light.

Darling,

There aren't enough street lights in the world for that kind of space.

There I was—
your beautiful fool,
slowly figuring out
how to help you.
How to comfort you.
And as time passed,
our friendship leveled out
as though there had never been
any hurtful moments between us.

The slate was as flat as the parking lot we stood in.

You'd think I would have learned
that nothing beautiful
could ever come
from dead, suffocated land.

But there you were,
kissing me. Holding my hands.
Telling me that you cared about me.
And I believed it,
because with you,
my canary song flourished
and gave life to the cold concrete
I was destined to fall on.

You kissed me that night
and I heard fireworks.

Not because the kiss was anything special,
but because you were cliché
and waited for the show to start
so that when you told me you loved me,
I would want to make the moment perfect
and say it back—

even if I wasn't ready.

Frozen lips kiss corpses—
memories of past loves,
thawing hearts drowned in the lake,
slowing beats in a hollow cavity,
longing for spring to break through
the layers of ice you encased me in
before I could learn to swim to safety.

What is it you taste
when you kiss me?

Is it berries?
Or tea?
Or chocolate?

Perhaps it's the sweetness of forgiveness
mixed with the bitter summer's first peach.

Or maybe
I taste like her memory,
and that's why you kiss me so often.

Secrets kept in bathroom stalls,
quick changes behind frosted glass.
I am becoming someone new,
and yet, still, no one can see me.

I love you, yes.
Frightfully so.

*Pinus taeda*

*Picea abies*

Fallen

I remember the night I finally fell
in love with you. We were driving
on an empty highway under the
waning moon. You missed our exit,
but neither of us noticed until an hour
had passed. And when we realized
what had happened, we laughed. And
I thought right then and there: this
is the man I want to spend my life with.
I would gladly continue getting lost with him.

Well, Darling, I certainly did just that, didn't I?
I fell in love, and you took everything
you could, and then, more, until I had
nothing—not even my identity. Although,
I wasn't really lost. Simply...

stolen.

I suppose I should say that
my greatest fears are spiders
and people.

You see, Darling,
one has many legs,
and the other, many faces.

We walked the cobblestone path
like it was the *Yellow Brick Road,*
and for a moment, your eyes filled
with magic. But then we turned
the key to our new home, and
my eyes seeped back to sepia.

That's how it was.
After I moved our apartments
to the next town over on my own—
because you had other people to be with—
I kept trying to convince myself
that maybe this life, which was slowly turning
to black and white, was what we had dreamed of.
That maybe this was our movie—
the pin up and the greaser,
forever trapped in some second-rate musical
that would never live up to the classics
we wanted so desperately to be a part of.

You were hardly home,
and when you were,
you were too busy composing
some knock-off soundtrack to a life
that didn't include me.

I tried to dance with you twice.
You would see me swaying in the kitchen
as I cooked and baked,
and you would make your comments
about how nice it was to see me like that—
*The perfect vintage housewife.*
So one day, I held out my hands
and called you over.
You said you didn't dance, and I laughed,
and I tried to walk you through it.

I blame myself for trying.
If your stubborn mind couldn't be swayed,
how could your body ever follow?

You showed me your favorite movies
and talked the whole way through,
then got mad at me when I couldn't
tell you every specific detail you asked about after.

You decided, one day,
to make us breakfast.
I got the plate of burnt eggs
and dry French toast,
and the lecture on how
your cooking was superior.

I choked down the food
along with honest words.

You had me make breakfast every morning after that.

I've always loved flowers.

Do you remember, Darling,
how I would hang them to dry,
or press them between pages
rather than throw them away?

You thought it was silly.
I thought it was beautiful.
Little moments of time, preserved
between prose and tied with twine.

I suppose that's why you never bought me flowers —
you didn't want to encourage happiness in our home.

I want to hold you
in this moment.
Somehow seal our souls
so that one day,
years and years and years from now,
someone will stumble across our love
and understand
how difficult it is to care
for a man made of stone.

I was everything you wanted -
the presence in a room
that didn't turn heads out of envy,
but out of curiosity,
only haunting those who knew
I was there with them.

I was the lips that left marks
on crinkled napkins and whiskey glasses,
the eyes that faded to a blur
as soon as I passed.

I was the woman in the walls,
silently crying out for you to remember me
as my touch,
which was only known through glances,
laughed with your dreams
of the women you surrounded yourself with.

I was not beautiful.
I was not memorable.

I was forgettable to everyone who left
in search of something more than a small town
divided by cobblestone paths,
strewn with autumn foliage,
and ghost stories swinging from the rafters.

I will never be more
than a blurred frame
from an old film.
But you, Darling,
will replay every time
someone new asks my name
and grows short because I don't smile.

We stain memories like glass,
hoping to transform the
broken and tainted into
something more beautiful.

Fix your lipstick and find a smile.

A pained face is prettier painted.

When they're upset,
some girls eat
their feelings. I ate
my crow, and then lifted
my tongue to show you
I had swallowed every last bit.

We were magnificent,
you and I.
The picture-perfect couple
with bright smiles and hopeful eyes,
our arms linked as heels clicked
down Main Street. You would give
a small nod or wave to the elderly
couples passing by. To them,
we were a happy memory.
A true main attraction.
A splendor to behold in vintage fashion
and color-correcting makeup.

Why is it, Darling, that you only ever kiss me
after I'm gone? Is there a greater thrill
in chasing my memory than there is laying
with me? I bought myself flowers and
thanked you for them because you felt ashamed
for forgetting my birthday. And our anniversary.
And Valentine's day. Again.

What does it say about us,
that I mourn the flowers more than our love?

We danced in the shadows
of streetlights and movie marquees,
more afraid of the morning
than the rain and oncoming cars.

You held my waist,
and I held onto the moment,
because I was unsure
of how long you would love me.

You were a hurricane
in the dead of winter –
unexpected and devastating,
my tears mixed with your hot air.

How could I have been so foolish
to not have seen the destruction
that came with your dreams
as they ripped mine from their roots?

How fitting it is, then,
that we should end the same way -
you in the shadows, dancing with her,
and me, displaced come the dawn.

Tell me, Darling,
was it me that you loved?
Or the words Kitty Kallen sang,
which you used to string me along
like the words on this page
and the years wasted
on sun-bleached polaroids
and broken kitten heels?

A palm,
low on my back,
hardly touching bare skin.
I shudder,
almost forgetting to breathe—

a proud cliché
I'll pull from my memory
as the snow melts.

Perfect lovers made of glass
still cut lips when they kiss.

In time, both will shatter.

I heard the names of every woman
you've ever loved
in the songs you played.

I wondered when your keys would play mine.

That night,
you composed a new piece—

but the name was a stranger's.

I danced to it anyway,
hoping that it would all be okay.

I always told myself
that I wouldn't be the other woman.
Yet, somehow, I was.
I sat in front of the vanity and
watched through empty eyes
as I became the woman you wanted
instead of the woman I was meant to be.

I used to have dreams.
I used to share them with you,
and you would share yours with me,
and sometimes, those dreams would
be dreamt up together.

But then I woke up and realized
that the dreams I thought we were sharing
were anything but wonderful.

We go to bed in silence—
a headboard for a headstone,
buried in cold sheets,
and hoping that someone will mourn
what we no longer have breath for.

Open up old wounds like bottles of bourbon.
Let the stream trickle down your throat,
down your chin,
down your shirt,
pool on the floor by your feet—
you're not curing anything
by letting the burn linger.

You're only wasting alcohol.

I suppose that should speak volumes,
how you're so quick to drain a bottle—
so quick to drain me
of energy and money and emotion.
The chip on your shoulder
matches the ones on the walls.

Tell me, Darling—
how long until you realize
that your rose-colored glasses
are actually whiskey?

Did you know, Darling,
that a page can only hold so much ink
before it tears?

Before the weight of the words
pressed into its skin
becomes too much,
and the seams of the spine unravel?

I'm sure you mustn't have,
because if you did,
you wouldn't have bombarded my binding
with so much,
so often.

Our hands are folded
much like the pages
of the letters I have written.

But Darling,
what happens when it comes
time to open them?

How gently will you separate
yourself
from
me?

How long before I'm tucked away
in a box, under the bed,
only to be forgotten?

I long to dance again,
but the songs you play
have become faster than I can spin
before growing dizzy and falling—

my breath,
heavier than the silence that lays between us in bed.

At least the silence still holds me.

*Can we put the tree up tomorrow?*
*Since we're both off of work?*
*I can make cookies and put on*
*an old holiday record,*
*and we can watch* White Christmas *after?*

You said yes, but in the morning,
you left before I woke up.
When I asked you where you were,
you said you were with her.

So the following week, I asked,

*Can we put the tree up tomorrow?*
*Since we're both off of work?*
*I can make cookies and put on*
*an old holiday record?*

And you said yes again,
but when morning came,
you were off with someone else.

So the following weekend,
I asked once more.

*Can we put the tree up tomorrow?*
*Since we're both off of work?*
*I can make cookies?*

And you said yes,
but for a third week in a row,
I waited all day and night for you
to come home. But you didn't.
So the following week, I said,

*I'm putting the tree up.*

You did't say anything
when you left.
But when you came home,
close to midnight,
and saw the tree
decorated and covered in lights,
the neighbors heard you sing
a familiar song of anger.

I sat on the sofa with a bottle
of wine, losing myself
out the window in the reflection
of the Christmas tree lights.
I never really liked wine.

But you drank all of my whiskey,
and the Pinot Noir matched my lipstick.

Merry Christmas, Darling—

The halls are decked.

The boxes of packages are piling up by the door.

The lights are twinkling.

All you have to do is sign our holiday cards

that say "we hope you have a happy holiday season."

I long to be held by you,
but instead, I'm cradled
by unfamiliar shadows
whose words are a vice grip
around my tired, breathless lungs.

Because I loved you
with everything I was,
I let you transform me
into someone I didn't know.

Do you have any idea how hard it is
to learn to love a stranger
on top of learning to love yourself?

We sat on the sofa—
well, I sat. You had
your head in my lap
as you cried about how
it wasn't fair that your friends
from home were holding you
responsible for you actions.

Tell me, Darling,
how long have you been carrying
the chalk for your own outline,
and why has it taken me so long
to realize that you're so confident
in your ability to play the victim?

Well, allow me to let you in on a little secret, Darling -
at the end of the day, your fingerprints
will be the only ones found at the scene,
and you're not that great an actor.

Sometimes,
we break the silence.

More often,
the silence breaks us.

The most astonishing thing happened today,
Darling.


As I was getting ready,
I found myself
looking in the mirror,
and when I asked my reflection,


How do I properly love you?


the voice that left my lips, replying,


You are undeserving of love,


sounded exactly


like


yours.

They told me to find myself
a man who kisses
as though he were going off to war
in the morning.

Well, Darling,
you certainly kissed that way.

At least,
that's how I saw you kiss her
while I waited for you at the Homefront.

You smile at me
and my stomach fills with
butterfly corpses.

He's looking at rings for me
and lingerie for her.

Isn't that romantic?

Calloused hands on soft skin
sound romantic until you wake up
and realize that the callouses were made from working
another woman's body while you worked
on smiling through nights spent alone
in a bed meant for two.

I heard you talk in your sleep a total of four times:

The first was in April,
the year that we met.
You confessed your love to me,
and I pretended that I hadn't heard what you'd said.

The second was in February,
You proposed, and I asked if you had asked my father,
and when you said, *shit, no,*
I told you that was okay,
because neither of us were ready for marriage.

The third was September.
You said you couldn't wait to get away from it all,
how exhausting it was.
I agreed, tired of working double shifts
because you wanted to take extra days off
to spend time with the girls from work.

I heard you talk in your sleep a total of four times:

The fourth time was two weeks later.

You said her name
and then told her how stupid I was.
How easy it was to sleep with her.
How her body was better than mine.

And I suddenly realized that *I* was what
you couldn't wait to get away from.

You didn't deny it.
You didn't try to hide it.
You simply shrugged your shoulders
and left without a word,
leaving my body scattered
like debris after a storm,
haloed by shattered glass
and the sunrise.

And then you had the audacity to come back.

You said my heart was untamable.

Is that why you had to go out
and conquer so many other women
before climbing back into our bed?

If so, you were foolish in thinking
that way. My heart was yours when
it came to love. But you were greedy
and wanted full control over all of me—

and Darling, I refuse to make myself
a casualty of your cruelty.

Would you like to see a magic trick, Darling?

When you turn around,
and knock on the door three times,
I will have disappeared without a trace,
and you will be left here, wondering
what to do in an empty home,
left for an empty man
full of empty promises
and pretty illusions.

I walked through the door,
and was first greeted by the
pile of your dirty dishes,
overflowing from the sink
and onto the counter,
which I had asked you to take care of
as I left that morning.

Then I saw you,
snuggled up on the sofa
with her and two others.
You looked as though you'd forgotten
that I lived there too.

I introduced myself—
clearly, by your reaction,
I was a stranger to everyone.

She ignored me, got up,
and began picking up my decorations
while telling the others how
wonderful you were.

I said I was going to bed,
and that if you were so comfortable
on the sofa, you could spend the night there.

You could have at least taken care of the dishes first.

I hope
that when you taste her
honey, you keep her
safe in your arms
and protect her
from the relentless enemies
you brought into our bed.

After all— even a king sized mattress
runs out of room eventually.

I hope
that when you hear the song
you called ours, and hers, and theirs,
you wait
for the record to end
before beginning something new.

After all— it's only polite to wait for the song to finish before changing partners.

I hope
that you choose
to cherish commitment,
and practice your promises,
and remember
that a ring
is more than just a rock.

After all— I did.

I do.

I hope
that now that I am gone,
you will appreciate
the laughter of your lover
more
than you do
the giggle of giddy girls.

After all— she was one.

I hope
that when you smell lavender and poppies,
it brings you back
to the Italian countryside
and the lazy mornings
that never lived
outside of pillow talk.

After all— something has to keep our future company.

I hope
that when you see sunflowers
reaching up to the sky,
you lift your hands
and take hold
of the ones that need you
for the first time.

After all— one can only hold onto nothing for so long.

A
B
C
D
E
F
G
H
I've got a guy
who cannot stay true.

Persephone left Hades for six months of the year,
and he was still faithful and loving.

Funny—

I couldn't even leave you for a six hour work shift
without you running off to someone else.

You were making cookies with her
in my kitchen, and loudly telling her
about how when we made cookies,
I only let you stir in the chips.

I wonder where that lie will fall—
maybe in my hands, close to the burn mark
you made with the cookie sheet.
Or in the trash, with my dead grandmother's
bowls you broke for no reason.
Or in the utensil holder,
with my favorite wooden spoon,
splintered and unusable from your lack of caring.
Or in the cabinet, with the measuring cups I replaced
after you threw the first set out
instead of washing them.

Why are love songs
so often written about heartbreak?

Are you only here to compose
a melody that will be
stuck in my head, no matter
how faint it becomes?
Something for me to cry over,
night after night, again and again,
waking up to an empty bed
and ghosts of what could have been?

I'm not sorry to disappoint you,
but my voice will ring louder than yours,
and the ghosts are quite good at harmonizing.

My song is the one that will be haunting your memories.

You said I didn't try hard enough,
but oh, Darling, how wrong you were.

I tried and I tried to see anything other
than the truth, hoping that I was wrong,
and that you still loved me.

But no matter how much I gave,
how much I sacrificed for you,
every morning, when I would open
my eyes, you would be gone from our bed,
and in your place was a hollow shell,
shouting the truth while her name
slipped from your still sleeping lips.

You eat her pussy like pasta —
slurping and sucking,
getting mess all over your face and shirt
as you make unsavory sounds.

She seems to be enjoying herself, though,
so I suppose you both get off on being
carelessly sloppy.

Tell me, Darling,
when you leave our bedroom,
shall I hand you a napkin,
or shall I continue to pretend
that you're a gentleman with
some semblance of table manners?

*I'm going to Ohio.*
*To see Ally*
*Alone.*

I wonder if your current mistress
knows about your future one.

When I turned my key,
the door didn't budge.
When I knocked,
there was no answer.
When I called,
I was sent to voicemail after two rings.
When I slept in my car that night,
too exhausted to drive to a friend's house,
and feeling safer behind a gate
than locked inside with you,
I felt more warmth from the
December air than I had in months in our bed.

When I woke up the next morning
to her getting into the car parked
next to mine, my heart should have sank.

Instead, it stayed beating— a steady rhythm,
preparing me for the day's unspoken battle.

You called me a lost cause.
I suppose I am, in a sense.

Not because I will never
achieve anything in life,
or amount to anything spectacular—
as you told me quite often—
but because it is impossible
for a boy like you
to love a woman like me.

I shouldn't have to buy myself flowers.

I locked the doors every night
when you were too distracted
to slide the chain after coming home.
Neither of us said anything.
It was a mundane routine
we fell into all too quickly.
You would come home, shower,
get comfortable in the living room,
and leave me to lock myself in
with the monster I feared so much.

But then that night came.

Thirty minutes.

One hour.

Two hours.

When three hours passed,
I stopped trying to reach you.
I stood in front of the door,
wondering if I should slide the second lock.
Wondering if you would come home or not.

Four hours.

I slid the chain into place.

Perhaps my name was never meant to be
played by your keys.

It beats in a wild manner,
skipping scales
rather than resting and waiting
for you and your next command.

I made her uncomfortable?

*I* made *her* uncomfortable?

I came home from a sixteen hour day,
exhausted, and found you spread out
in the living room with all of our supposed friends,
drinking my whiskey and wasting my wine,
her wearing my shirt while sitting in your lap,
and *I* made *her* uncomfortable?

If she's going to make herself at home,
and take my things from my closet,
and my place in our bed,
she can pay my share of rent.

You were so obsessed with how your body looked
that you never saw how quickly you were rotting.

Your words festered under blistered skin
and your face scarred with names from the past.

Your breath reeked of alcohol and vomit,
and her, of course,
but you still expected me to kiss you
and call you handsome.

You saw me as a painted accessory,
dolled up for you to show off.
But as soon as another woman came around,
you dropped my hand and turned away.

You told me you wanted to be proud of me,
and that I had to work out and lose weight,
and wear this blouse with that skirt,
and then got angry with me because I didn't.

Well, Darling,
allow me the chance to explain:

kitten heels and cardigans are impractical attire
for cleaning up your messes,
and how could I possibly have the energy
to go to the gym after working to support you,
and carrying the weight of our relationship
and your drunk body up three flights of stairs?

Your fingertips say, *I love you.*
Your lips say, *don't leave me.*
Your eyes say, *I'm sorry*

You're speaking a language you only partially understand,
letting empty words seep through closed teeth
like a last minute memorization of a movie script,
hoping that they latch on to guilt,
or regret, or what little love you think I have left for you.

I can tell that you don't quite know
what, exactly, it is that you're hearing
come out of your mouth,
so allow me to translate,
because I am fluent in forgotten:

Your fingertips say,
*I want to touch someone, and she's not here right now*

Your lips say,
*I'm too drunk to move, and too embarrassed to have her
see me like this.*

Your eyes say,
*I need you to clean up another one of my messes.*

I say, *no*, and suddenly,

Your fingertips say, *no one else will ever love you.*
Your lips say, *you don't have a choice in leaving.*
Your eyes say, *I'm sorry I was caught.*

When I open my mouth to translate again,
you still don't understand,
so please be patient with me
while I try a few more languages:

*You do not control me.*

*You do not own me.*

*I feel sorry for you.*

*I do not love you.*

*I deserve better.*

*Goodbye.*

Do you see it, darling?

Just there, on the horizon?
The storm that's building up
faster than your pile of lies and secrets?

That's the freedom of finally leaving you.

*One last kiss?*
you asked.
The clock struck midnight.
The neighbors hooted and cheered.
I saw no sorrow in your eyes.
I kissed you anyway.

And when I pulled back
from the empty, depressing peck,
I saw that you understood—

I had kissed you
the same way you had been kissing me
since you started kissing her.

You tell me that I'm too much.
That I'm too much to love.
Too much to handle.
Too much of—
you wave your hands in the air.

*If I'm too much,*
*then go and find less.*

You freeze at my words.
I know you're expecting a fight.
That's what you do.
You gaslight those around you until
they blow up in your face
and you have enough debris
to bury yourself as the victim.

*If I'm too much,*
*then go and find less,*

I repeat.

*Go find someone*
*who will do less.*

*Who will care for you less.*

*Who will love you less.*

*Because I love myself too much*
*to let you try to make me any less of a woman.*

Bruise-branded
and alone.
Peel off the thin facade.
Remember that he will never see
the true worth of your heart.

Today is the day you choose yourself.

Quercus rubra

Quercus velutina

Quercus douglasii

Flying

I woke up on the sofa the next morning.
I made tea and picked up a book,
set on enjoying my day off,
when you asked if we could talk.

I tilted my head back,
indifferent to anything you had to say.

*I've decided I'm gonna start dating Marissa.*

I didn't flinch.
I didn't react.
You didn't get mad.
That part surprised me.

*Okay then.*

You waited for me to react,
and when I didn't, I simply continued,

*That's not news,* ~~████████~~
*You started dating her months before we broke up.*

That part surprised you.

Looking at it all now,
the most hurtful thing
you did was interrupt my reading.

*I only cheated because I thought you were cheating on me.*

No. No you didn't.

You cheated because I got tired
of being your little doll.
Tired of being a maid.

You think I cheated?
The only thing I cheated was time,
working three jobs in one day
on top of grad school, and cooking,
and cleaning, and making sure that
when I was done washing her lipstick
out of your shirt collars, I had enough
common sense not to confront you.

You moved into the spare room after that.
I kept the master— after all, the lease was in my name.

I got myself a bed— one that you would never sleep in.
I arranged everything to feel more like a sanctuary
and less like a holding cell. A simple desk and shelf.
Small, round tables in two of the corners, stacked with plants.
Curtains framed the window, which stayed open for the light.
Painted wood housed sketches on book pages. A small dresser.

Gone were the days of a king bed blocking the window.
Gone were the days of bare walls.
Gone were the days of feeling like a stranger in my home.

But most importantly,
gone were the days with you.

There was a painting your mother gave us—
I believe your grandmother or great-grandmother painted it,
although I could be mistaken. But it was from someone
in your family. Your step-father hung it above my bed
when they came to visit, not long after I ended things with you.
It was of a house in a clearing in the woods.
Pink and blue and ivory flowers blossomed in the trees and bushes,
surrounding it in soft, painted streaks of light. Everything
about that piece was bright and calm— except for the windows.
Those were cold, and dark, and empty.

Every now and then,
I could have sworn
I saw someone pass
behind those windows
as if to say, *you're not alone.*
*You're not the only ghost*
*this family has. But you*
*will live— not trapped,*
*but flying freely*

I miss that painting more than you.

I miss your mother and step-father more than the painting.

I sat on the sofa,
cutting lace for a dress
you would never see me in.

Peach, sage, pink—
flowers, leaves, a scalloped edge
falling gently over my knee as
I hummed to one of my records,
head tilting this way and that.

You put the television on
and sat next to me, uninvited.

*Isn't this nice?*
*Us coexisting?*

I didn't look up from my work.
*I suppose. But I was existing*
*perfectly fine before you came back.*

I counted the days until the lease was up
and I could finally be rid of you.

Your car pulled up next to mine
in the neighboring lane at the red light.
I was laughing, singing along to a favorite song,
dancing a little in my seat.
You never really saw that side of me.
That's when you blasted some sad country song
and rolled down your windows, getting me to look.

Then the light turned green,
and I turned the corner,
and you were left under another light.

The door slammed shut behind you.
I was so used to the noise, though,
that I didn't jump or flinch.
I heard your boots on the floor come to a stop.
You fell to your knees and begged me,
in the middle of the living room,
to give you a second chance.
And when I said No, you broke down crying.
You weren't upset because of my answer –
you were upset because you knew
I wasn't under your control anymore.

But Darling, I'll let you in on a little secret.

As much as I hate to admit it,
even with you curled up at my feet,
in that moment,
you still made me feel small.

You love me?
How unfortunate.

You won't make it without me.
You'll be lost without me.
Unknown without me.
You're weak without me.
You need me.

Me...
Me...
You never thought of me, did you?
You never said my name, in or out of bed,
unless you were angry with me,
because outside of anger,
you couldn't keep track of your women,
could you, Darling? You were too scared
that you would call me someone else,
and I would find out before you could
get your stories straight. You never considered
me and what I might enjoy on the far and few
dates we went on, or how I would get home
after you left me to go be with your friends.

You never considered how I might feel
on the other side of your temper tantrums,
and accusations, and broken promises and plates.

Call me selfish, if you must, but I am only
thinking of myself now. And Darling,
despite what you may think,
I am the most dangerous one in this room.
I am a woman who survived living in your world.
My body stands tall now, and blocks out your artificial light.
My bones are no longer weary, but rooting into the earth
and growing into winding branches
for swings instead of nooses,
covered in leaves instead of leavings.

Spring came back into my life
when I left you and your Winter.
There is color, and hope, and beauty again.

And one day, when life finally fucks you,
you will scream my name.

I thought that,
after all you had
taken from me,
I would have nothing
more to give—

I was wrong.

What I have now
are my words,
which have been gathered
and assembled with love
for those who will read them
instead of you.

I helped convince your mother
to have you bring your new love
home for an "extended vacation"
when she said she wanted me to come.

Maybe waiting the lease out
wouldn't be so hard after all.

All I wanted— all I really wanted—
when we moved into a place of our own
was to have friends over for dinner.
I would set the table with a nice tablecloth,
and take out the good dishes, and arrange fresh flowers
in the center of the table. Instead, you covered
it with your toys and trash, and got mad when
I asked you to clean up your things.

The first thing I did
when you walked out the door
to go back to Louisiana with her
was clear that damn table.

And what a wonderful three months it was—
you with her, and me, eating dinner at a table
for the first time in over two years.

But then you said you were coming back,
and that she was moving in,
and I knew things would get worse.

The room was empty.
Nothing in the closet.
Nothing in the bathroom.
Nothing.
Not even dust, dancing in the light.
Just air.
Just space.
And for the first time in years,
I was able to breathe easily.

Freshly chipped nails
fold papers, tucked away between
book pages as the sun sets—
golden light shadowing
figures on the other side of open windows.

I hear a love song
and think of you.
Of how we could have been
something worth memorizing.

Then I fold another paper,
tuck my book into my bag,
and smile, because after this fleeting moment,
you will no longer be worth my future.

Merry Christmas, Darling.

The halls are bare.

The boxes of my belongings are piling up by the door.

The lights are turned off.

All I have to do is sign the letter

that says I won't be renewing the lease
after the holiday season.

It's ironic, isn't it?
For me to immortalize you
in these pages,
dedicating a part of my heart
to someone who cared
so little for it.

Maybe that's why
I will never let your name
run rampant
through these lines.

Because as long as you
have no true hold
on my words, I can
continue to write
about every heartbreak
you caused me.

About every broken promise,
every missed date night,
every shattered dream
you made me sweep up
from the floor by your feet.

And as the ink leaves
my memory, I can love
myself more and more.

You unleashed dragons,
thinking I would look to you
for protection.

Pity you didn't realize
I was strong enough
to save myself.

Brush your thumb
over my words
and bring my memory
to your mouth
like parted lips, begging for breath.
Don't worry— I'm not
a poison, poised to kill.
Instead, my words will linger
in your head—
a sweet, silken voice
on the edge of hope—
and you will know
that a poet's love
will either breathe in
life, or fester the
corpse of your name.

If I was your muse,
then you were a thief.
You stole my name,
my body, even my heart
for a short while.
But Darling, you
will never steal my soul.

There is no canvas in this world
strong enough to hold it —
no medium bright enough
to capture its true essence.

My heart beats,
not for you,
but for myself.

Listen to my war drum,
announcing my arrival
to the long overdue battle
for my body.

I don't quite know who I am
or what I'm doing.

I had an idea, once.
A dream.
But Darling, you told me that it was a foolish,
fleeting notion -

much like a snowfall in June:

silly and utterly impossible.

But that's the best part of life, sometimes, isn't it?

The dreaming.

I wanted to thank you for never loving me
enough to write a song for us.

You see, Darling,
while your hands were shaking at the keys for her,
mine were steady enough to open the door

and leave.

Keep your love songs.

I will keep my promises.

You tried to lead our dance,
but ended up pulling me along,
not caring that I stumbled across the dance floor
as you made your way to a new partner
before the song had even ended.

How magical it was, then,
to hear a melody playing from the distance,
your drowning voice and sickly lyrics
tuned out behind closed doors.

How surprising it was,
to discover that the melody was mine.

I wonder, Darling,
when the mist settles
and the dawn breaks through,
cascading warm rays over the day,
will you look to find me
and be greeted with the same coldness
I have felt for so long now?

Why does the world stop turning
for someone so insignificant?

I don't think it does—
not really.
I think that you made me feel
like I was nothing without you.
And when my world began to shatter,
I ignored the cracks in the compass,
because you said you were my home,
so what need had I for leaving?

But then the glass broke free
of its metal confinement,
and it filled the air with crystals
that glistened in the sunlight
you had blocked out for so long.

The world didn't stop turning because of you, Darling.
The world keeps turning in spite of you.
The world keeps turning, spinning,
along with a restless needle,
leading me to every fantastic love story
this healing heart can hold.

I think I know why
it was so difficult for you
to put my name to music—

I refused to be a continuation
of every fleeting love before me,
and you only know how to play one song.

To fall in love
with someone's writing
is to fall in love with their soul.

You said that I was illegible.

Perhaps you were just illiterate.

Do you still have the love
letters I wrote to you?
The ones I kissed,
leaving lipstick stains
where the postage stamp should have gone?

I would like them back now.

Come winter, I'll use them to help start a fire,
and then, maybe,
I'll finally feel some warmth from you.

What I will miss most, Darling,
is waking up to you,
fiddling away at your piano,
meticulous melodies polluting the air
with the most beautiful lies.

Tell me, Darling,
if your hands couldn't reach
the opposite ends of your keys,
how did you ever expect to reach the hand
being held out next to you?

*I love you,* no longer
comes with runny mascara
and gaslit apologies.

*I love you,* no longer
spends restless nights
waiting for you to come home.

*I love you,* no longer
blindly washes out
lipstick stains on your collar.

*I love you,* no longer....
*I love you,* no longer....

Well, it's as simple as that, really:

*I love you no longer.*

There will be no post cards from foreign countries,
scented with French perfumes
and kissed in the corner.

No souvenirs brought back,
and no stories to share over day-old take out.

You see, Darling,
after all of this traveling,
I have realized that
I am homesick for everyone and everything

except for you.

I used to wish that you would see me
looking up at the stars and fall
in love with me. A true love,
not one built from anger and selfishness.

Now I hope that you look up at the stars
and know that I am perfectly happy
without you.

You told me that I would never find
a love like yours again.

But don't you see, Darling?
That's the point.

I want to find a love like mine.

The marks you left
on my skin
may have become
invisible,
but the scars
on my bones and heart
will ring though legends
long after I have gone.

You said that my wings were weak—
damaged, thin, and torn.

Look again, closer this time.

My wings have carried me here.
There is beauty in every scar,
in every tear.

How strong they must be,
to still flutter after so much pain.

That's the beauty of it all—
the burning pages,
the scorched photos,
the ash floating in the sunbeams.

Come morning,
all I have to do is sweep you up
and be rid of you.

How lovely it would have been,
to go our separate ways as friends,
and then, one day, by fate or chance,
see each other again and smile
from across a hallway as you played
your piano for the crowds. And with
each step I took towards you, I would
dance, and you would play faster.

But Darling, that was your dream.
A way for you to feel at peace
with me leaving you behind. In
your dreams, I am the villain and you
are conducting a life filled with such
passion and fierceness.

How serendipitous, then, that I did
see you the other day. You did not
see me, though – I made sure of that.
You don't get to spend a moment more
hearing my laughter or watching me smile.

My happiness and future are no longer
tied to you. Yours, however, will always
be tied to me. You see, Darling,
I recognized the song you were playing.

My name was finally on your keys –
heavy, regretting, and far more loving
than you ever were towards me
when I was yours.

There was love in these walls—
long ago.
Back before the earth ever broke.
When the foundation was a dream,
drawn out in black and white.

There was love in each nail,
in each board, and each tile—
a palace that lived in ideas,
constructed from the best of intentions.

There was love in the laughter,
sliding down the bannisters,
looking out the windows at daisies.

There is still love here,
so many years later.
It collects dew drops
in the form of spiderwebs,
tucked away in the rafters.
It sings in the shape of wind
during late spring days when
a storm is on its way. It stands,
silently, in every shadow cast
by cloth-covered tables and
broken dishes, whose patterns
are scattered about the floor,
matching the dried flowers in
antique vases from way back when.

Your idea of love left us in ruin,
but mine will haunt the day's last light.

Bare feet tiptoe as hips sway
to an ending record. Red lips
are washed away, along with
perfume, worn at your request.
Petticoats and linen dresses
are replaced with silk and lace.
Wild curls cascade over bare breasts,
free from suffocating pins and spray.
Pearls scatter on a hardwood floor,
rolling into constellations in candlelight,
reminding us that new beginnings
often start with broken strands.

I am most intimate
with my ghosts—
the different versions
of myself from the days
when I didn't know my name,
or what I could do
if I just let my lungs breathe.
Versions who once loved you
instead of me.
These ghosts sing songs
of childhood while we tend
to each other's wounds
and smile sympathetically,
trapped in ornate mirrors.

I know what they're thinking.
After all of the sleepless nights,
and spilled tears chasing wine,
and silent arguments,
they're wondering when I will
join them, and another
will come and take my place.

One of the most painful things
a person can do is lie
to themself— let themself down.

But today, I will do just that.
Today is the day
I will open the windows
and let the lost souls out.

I'm putting on my makeup,
and suddenly, it's Christmas again,
and I'm painting on my smile
and acting out the lies
you forced me to tell our families.

And then I laugh,
because today,
in this moment,
all I can think is
how wonderful it is
to not waste perfectly good lipstick
on you.

I have often found that the best love stories
are those we find in books.

If we're lucky, we will find someone
who brings about that feeling outside the pages.

Darling, my world did not end with you.
You were merely the prologue
to my greatest adventure.

I left you,
and time continued on.
I traveled with it to cities and mountains,
across oceans, and to the edges of fjords,
before finally returning home.

My toes dug deep into the familiar earth,
and the crickets serenaded the moon and me,
and come morning's eye,
my willing heart exhaled—

completing my first moment as the woman
I had been searching for.

There are days when the clouds bow to the sun
and the oceans look like scattered stones.

There are days when morning breaks
and the mist carries whispered secrets.

There are days when the flowers sing
and the sparrows sweep away stardust.

But Darling —
gone are the days when I loved you.

My heart is beating now that you're gone—

I was left with the ghosts of us
and of what could have been,
showing me the wonder of a day
where the sun shines on my shadows.

How I love the dawns without you.
How I love the dusks with myself.

Now I know how the moon feels
after she has been eclipsed.

She is awake now, Darling, but is too tired
to rise on her own, so I will climb the trees
with her in hand, and you, back on the ground,
fondly forgotten just beyond midnight.

I couldn't be your savior,
but I could save
myself from you.

Tomorrow, I will love myself
just a little bit more.

I speak in rain
and bloom with the flowers
as the dusk sends quiet hope
across indigo fields.

The fireflies and the carpenter bees
dance with me in the meadow
as memories of you
drift away with the tides.

There's a silent understanding
between the earth and me.

She embraces my heart
in a way you never could.

I have found a fire that matches mine
in the honest breaths of nature. In the cracks of
ivy-covered stone and open fields at sunrise.
I am wonderfully unrooted among the wildflowers,
hopping on rocks to cross rivers, and burying
your memory far away from the birds who did
not survive the winter, out of respect for them.
Yes. I have found a fire that matches mine.
Our sparks scatter into the night sky, burning ash
like stars and lighting up the darkness
you tried so hard to keep me trapped in.

I spent so long in the cold
that my words fell like soft snow.
Flurrying around us— gentle,
fleeting, and all together, unremarkable.

But to him, every *I love you*
is a fractal-frozen fjord at sunrise,
beaming warmth into a new day,
and melting away the promise of darkness.

He doesn't try to play me on an instrument.
He doesn't write me down and scratch me out on paper.
He isn't unhappy with what he's failed to make me—
he wants me as I am.

He holds my face between his hands,
exhales with a kiss,
and lets go to watch me dance,
following beside me,
eagerly awaiting what we will create
together.

I will not forgive you.

I will not forgive you for what you did,
or what you said,
or how you treated me.

But I will forgive myself for not leaving sooner.

To you,
I was a cold and distant thing,
inching closer to lifelessness
with every step away from you.
You thought that my existence
was for compliments and kisses—
the words just as empty as the actions—
but you didn't mind because
I was obedient and quiet,
and where I settled, you easily found
someone reaching to make up for
the empty space in bed.

How beautiful that love was—
that I wanted to protect myself
from you so desperately,
that I let you ruin me
until I could safely escape
and begin to heal.

Loving myself
after you
has been my greatest act
of self destruction.

Letters to...

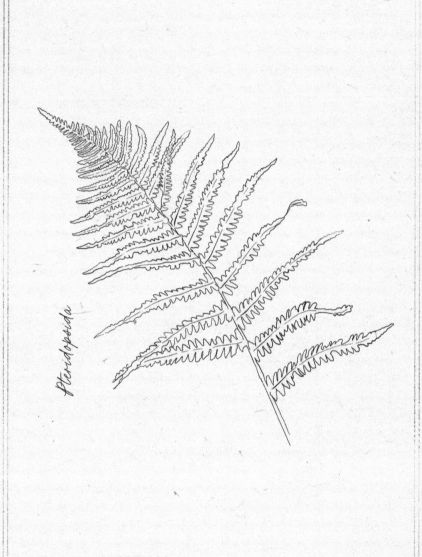

Pteridopsida

Dear Darling:

Forward To: The Woman You Are Loving Now

I hope that you're enough—

not for him, but for yourself,

so that one day, if he grows up

and realizes what it truly means

to love someone other than himself,

he will properly cherish you,

and the pain of your overlapping

time with me will have been worth it.

*Helianthus*

Dear Darling:

Forward To: The Woman You Will Love Next

I hope that you're rolling your eyes

and huffing in the frustration

that comes with reading a second letter.

But whether or not you're the same reader as before—

I hope that you're the last woman for him.

I hope that you have a life filled with love

and respect, and that he has finally learned

what it means to be a partner.

Rosa hybrida

Dear Darling:

Forward To: The Woman You Loved Before Me

If you're anything like me,
you would have thought that,
for a brief moment, at least,
he was the greatest
love of your life. That what you shared
was what Hollywood made films about,
what bards and crooners sang of,
and what the great poets and playwrights
penned on parchment to share with the world.

If you are anything like me,
you would have realized that he was the greatest
disappointment of that time of your life,
as he could love no one other than himself,
but pretended to, because you were strong,
and kind, and dreamt of something more—
something he wanted, but could never have.

I hope that you have found the romance
you once thought you shared with him.
I hope that you find it over oceans and fjords,
in vineyards and at the peaks of mountains.
I hope that you find what you thought you felt
in every dusk and dawn and midnight dance.
I hope that you find it in yourself
and the passing glances from souls trapped in time.

I hope that you have found a love to outlast history.

Paeonia lactiflora

Dear Darling:

Forward To: The One I Loved After

Thank you for showing me what love really was—
and with it, great heartbreak.

The kind that begins as familiarity
in a stranger's eyes,
and turns into scattered small talk
that, one day, takes over an entire day
and the night that follows.

The kind of love that builds with each sunrise.
That doesn't waiver as the night folds in,
instead, finding new beauty in each constellation
in the sky, and in the freckles on
shoulders, and cheeks, and thighs.

The kind of love that makes your helpless heart
believe again. The kind of love that
shatters you when you realize
it will never be anything more than what it already is.

And so it slowly fades back, not in actions,
but in days. The kisses never weaken.
The touches continue to linger.
The nights, warmer. Until the sunrise fades
the moments to memories,
and memories become favorite chapters in
familiar books with worn bindings.

To the love that was as true a love
as this world could offer.

Thank you for breaking my heart
without breaking me.

*Rosa rubiginosa*

Dear Darling:

Return To Sender


There is a difference

between loving recklessly

and loving selfishly.

I used to think that they were the same—

that selfishness lead to recklessness.


I see now, that they are so very different.


He loved you recklessly,

and in doing so, you were lost—

not only to him, but to everyone else.


You loved yourself selfishly,

and are all the better for it.

*Dear Reader,*

Thank you for holding my words
in your hands and in your heart.

If you have come to know my darling,
or someone like him,
I hope that my words help you keep your voice.
I hope that you are never silenced,
and that one day, you will find a love like yours.

Please remember to love yourself selfishly,
and those around you with all you can.

Love may end, love may fail, but love
will also come again.

When it does, I hope that you embrace it
with everything you are—

be it a person, a place, or a dream.


With every speck of stardust,


*Freydis*

Your Letters

# ACKNOWLEDGEMENTS

---

To Momma and Dad,
Thank you for encouraging me to share my words
with the world, and believing in every silly, little
dream of mine— even when I didn't.

To Rachel S.,
Thank you for being my sister and best friend, and
for standing by me from the beginning to the end of
this chapter in life. I can't wait to see what our next
adventure is.

To Antoinette and Tracy,
Thank you for being my secret keepers, for all of the
late night talks, and for helping me catch my footing
after slaying dragons.

To Rachel C.,
I never imagined that my words would make it to
print. Thank you for patiently helping me with this
process. There is no one I would trust more with my
words than you.

To Laura,
Your soul is as beautiful as your sister's. Thank you
for being one of my closest friends. I wish we had
the chance to know each other earlier.

To Dawn and Scott,
Thank you for loving me through everything.
I miss you both dearly.

And finally, to *you*.

## About the Author

The work of poet and artist Freydis Lova dances between the sorrow and ecstasy of life, revealing a myriad of nuances surrounding the human condition and what it means to be alive— all wrapped up in a comforting blanket of gentle metaphor and engaging prose.

Lova has earned five degrees in higher education, and has an extensive background in the English language arts. She is an accomplished editor and lifelong learner— ever fascinated by this world.

She is currently based in the American Northeast— living in a little house near a meadow of enduring wildflowers, a forest of lost trails, and a sea, surely filled with mysteries.

### Also by Freydis Lova

*The Traveler's Journals*
Volume I: Rinascimento

9 798987 338810